The Hell Inside Us
Weasel

Author: Weasel

Title: The Hell Inside Us

© 2015 Weasel
http://poetweasel.weebly.com

Published through Earl of Plaid Press
http://www.earlofplaid.com/

Table of Contents

"Walk through this with me. Through this church birthed of blood and muscle where every move our arms take, every breath we swallow is worship. Bend with me. There are bones in our throats. If we choke it is only on songs."

—Anis Mojgani

"I no longer need you to fuck me as hard as I hated myself."

—Buddy Wakefield

"The weight of the world is love."

—Allen Ginsberg

"We draw our strength from the very despair in which we have been forced to live. We shall endure."

—Cesar Chavez

"Your mind will answer most questions if you learn to relax and wait for the answer."

—William S. Burroughs

Adam

my notebook is the name
of every dude
i ever wanted to fuck,
slowly diminishing, turning
rational thinking into typewriter
bullets about getting close to
living; putting horses to rest
after running them dry.

pages filled with stuffed paranoia
making the ground harder when
you fall face first into the hot
asphalt, but bruises are a sign of
bravery, wounds from chances
you invested time in. sometimes,
it pays to get a little fucked up.

there's poetry inside us all,
crack open your ribcage and strike
a match against your heart, you'll
see the caveman drawings tattooed
along yourself, early innovations
of your story held up and archived
on your flesh, letting you know that
you still don't know you're amazing;
that you can do anything.

so i left my prayer beads at the altar
of all my midnight explorations,
giving thanks to the dead stories
they have left me with, but there are
no mantras for the dead. i still spill
ink to them some nights, as they
light fuses to shoot rocks through our
past. broken muses plaguing 4AM
words thrown onto paper, breaking
stillness with the calamity clack clack
clack of the keyboard. fully automatic
words deriving from the empty spaces
not yet filled in my bones.

burning cigarettes on my forearm,
i have named them Adam, second
chance deliriums injected into my
veins. we drift from each other, though
i offer up sacrifices of myself so i can
pen my thoughts into him, but i am still
searching for the crossroads of our story.

Philosophy

Piggly
Piggly wiggly
Piggly wiggly squiggly winks!

Such an odd combination of words.
I doubt there's anyone that can tell me what they
mean. And before anyone can jump up in
enlightenment, let me tell you that I know what they
mean.I'm the one that gave them meaning;
that took pen to paper and said:

The words are as holy as the Bible itself
No offence.

Great Jesus, Piggly Wiggly Squiggly Winks.

Words are words,
stretching from our tongues—
meanings outsourced; only
we are from a whole other universe.
There's still days where can't understand ourselves.

We throw words like knives,
Expect people's skin to be thicker but
our skin is not a wall to keep us
from going over the edge.

When I was first called a faggot,
I felt the blades of every letter.
The T was the first flesh wound
draped across my cheek. I

was less of a human. Made into
wandering skin-suit, dancing
panic attacks to get through
the hallways.

I still remember cigarette
burns on the floor; the
prayers unanswered—the
ambience of patience.

I became a terrorist when
I allowed myself to become
less of a man, and being less
of a man means that you are unhuman. That
god, does not smile upon your misfortunes.

Piggly flop
Piggly drop
Piggly stop
N O T H I N G

I know that you all have questions,
that's why you're looking at me like
I'm crazy, but it's not crazy to
believe that words are collected by
every one of us.

But words are words, and the
meanings are of an entirely different universe.
There are still days we can't understand them.

These Things Will Pass

my father told me that
he didn't recognize faggots
as people; that animals
must pray to find forgiveness.

so each night i wrote my prayers
in a notebook, ripped them
out and allowed the words to
scar my insides. i was told that
if you sat still long enough
the ink would heal all wounds.

it only made me sick;
only made me break the
towers i forced my arms
to build, realizing that we
have all forgotten our god.

we allow our hearts to be
filled with pistols and brimstone,
shooting the doves inside
our children. innocence is a
doctrine burned from our bodies.

dreaming is a forgotten luxury,
the soft persuasion that understood
our wounds; that understood the
cuts inside us when absolution never came.

at night i pull words from my veins,
lay them like body bags on the ground

allowed them to spread roots in the dirt;
my own scripture singed to the grass.

these words are my ghosts. painted
doors etched upon their chests, not
ready to reveal how desolate they've
become. the ashes of their sins still
stuck in the silos of their broken throats.

the stars we sit beneath are labyrinths
to our dreams,reminders that
papercut wounds are not scars;
that these wavering prayers shall pass.

liminality

my family never believed
in forgiveness. they only
chattered about exile because
such warmth could not be afforded.

there is too much earth
in my heart; too much dirt
collecting between the veins
as its beat soothes burnt pages
from tattered memoirs that
i never wanted to remember.

my closet never had a
door, but it was still
easy to hide the scars
away from knowing that
love had fallen too far from the edge.

i never had the right to
sorrow; realized that being
fair to oneself was not the
same as being alive.

poems were the prayers
that told me there still another
sunrise; that it only took a little
heat to understand that
ashes are not permanent.

take the pages kept hidden--
the piece of yourself locked

in boxes--and toss them into
the world. draw a heart on your
hand and show that we are all
not that different; that love
isn't always a mistake.

Byzantium

He was the only cancer who wanted more than to be someone's fuck toy; hair lashing his face as the breeze rushed through the buildings he passed by. It appeared the stranger had been waiting at the end of his lifetime for a long while. The wrinkles on his face formed roadmaps to wishes that died in the caverns of the man's memories—wishes of nowhere. He never walked in beauty, only with beauty when he could afford the grace to do so. He was never loved and no one ever told him he needed to love to keep his mind from wandering away from the clenches of sanity. So he picked up whoever he could, a few anonymous sperm donors to keep him company in the late ours of the morning, carrying him off into the stairs of his apartment and sucking the romance off their dicks. There are ghosts in the air that wait around to hear the novels of our weeping. They caught his tears, helping him to build a metropolis of forgiveness inside him. He granted their mercy all too often because everything about him was absolution. Taste of his flesh and drink of his body, the sins of his companions cleansed away in one full climax. Confession is over at dawn. At night he still dreams of walking off to the only mecca he can feel; the only place that continues to die off inside him—nowhere.

Falling Among Stars

we never danced, along her waters
we never smiled among her tears
trickling down, our footsteps totter
stairs between her stars.

you split my heart.
right from the start.
you catch as i'm falling
down her shores afraid...

      but...

I'm here, whispering in your ear
I'm here, whispering in your ear.

there's an apology sitting along the steps of my spine.
it's words make their home in my veins, sprouting
roots to paper in hopes that it will one day mingle
with your blood; that it will one day light itself on
fire
to stimulate the poetry that's been lost
between the silos of your ribcage.

you dripped morphine into your flesh. you told
me it kept you alive; that it kept the sun
from burning your skin. i watched as the roadmaps
in your eyes slowly diminished. vagabond roads
turned to shattered alleyways in the rain;
fears subsided into the abyss with each
                    muzzling
                       shot.

you stared at the moon, asked me about the
waters along her surface and the stars were sprawled
among the background. i told you they were
simply her oceans escaping the craters
that lay naked above us.

how i wish i could squeeze the
venom from your body,
hang you along the clothesline and watch
you come back anew. but i am merely human.
i could only wrap myself around you like weeds
in hopes that you were sober enough from
following the ghosts in the skies. you were
already there, lingering like cigarette smoke,
                    drifting
                         with the
                              clouds.

numb

look at the ocean above us—
wild, the clouds clench together,
holding its poise to give us
the comfort that's been missing.

to free us of the belief that every
jackal is a curse; that the right verse
and the right prescriptions allow us to breathe.

and though the west is slowly closing,
the damned have never received
such relief as it holds their cries,
cradling them—building a wall
around the history they carry.

the clouds release, letting out a sigh;
out of the solemnity its breath
reaches the ground. *we don't dream often enough.*

You

there's a man in the floor above me
shouting cocaine-driven obituaries
at the sun, believing that one day
his words will have so much force
that they'll come to life. he is at
the point where rational conversations
end, getting wrapped up in his paranoia,
while draining dreams through a/c vents.

every morning i hear him, forgetting where
his home is, forgetting that something can
exists outside of you, the cannonball memory
he has yet to shoot out, waiting to lick the
footsteps off the ground when you return to him.

there are labyrinths between his fingers, holding
nothing more than doped up deliriums contracted
by your hands, freedom he can cling too.

i want to talk with him, but i only know
directions on how to forget, and he is
not ready for that path; he still follows
alleyways that carry your scent, not
knowing that he'll never find you, that
you have dissolved yourself from him.

early morning winds howl at the window,
his mantras rising in the east, warming the
frost away at the illusion of your presence.

one day, he'll forgive himself and remove
the devastation from his voice.

Fixation

he loved the way that you moved
the way your feet caressed the sands
never leaving an ounce of yourself
how it screamed: "did you miss me?"
and he was still able to follow

I remember the nights
you would lay out and stare back at the stars
you only wanted to escape for a little while
to leave his voice behind

how many tears has the sun caught from your face?
How many cities have been flooded
by the empty droplets released from your eyes?

they're not so hidden anymore

Grace

he touched her spine,
cradling a new note as his hands
arched along the curve of his lover's
back. Her body lay against him
slowly coiling around to meet him amidst the sun.

she, was his obsession—the novel
etched around his ring finger after she
padlocked him in her asylum;
hips could never break a man so quickly.

hell was never for children but
for him who can forgive though never
allow himself the smile of forgiveness.

her bones were an orchestra
waiting for the gasoline to
come alive; his brittle
fingers only scratch at
her surface before the fire never starts.

Requiem

there is a comfortable silence in the late hours; a lost
peace only the insomniacs understand. midnight is
the apple from the wrong tree, but is eaten because
sacrifice is an addiction only we can explain. a ritual
lulling our hearts as we appease the questions that
have filled our bellies. nirvana as it lays.

i am driving under broken streetlamps when i see
them, local street ninjas uncovered sensually by the
headlights in the frozen ohio air. passing good times
and nicotine through huddled flesh. they slowly
dissolve into the darkness of the sidewalks, eyes
locking as i maneuver my way through, dreams
opening doors painted with paths neither of us
wanted to delve in to.

he is only a house away, the temptation that has
ripped away my personal eden, waiting for us to
follow the stars to their graves so we can be reborn.
he is a labyrinth my hands grow anxious to explore.
tonight he is holy, filled with a decadence i have not
yet tasted, and this odyssey can only be made once in
a person's lifetime. we have hated ourselves just long
enough to drive into the same black hole of freedom.

i trudge through the snow with an appetite greater than the dope they are selling to each other, trading personal requiems for quick fixes and pale stories. it is not what i desire, and in all our dreams we come to know this, and we wait to experience.

fedora

there's a hat in my closet.
it carries the solemnity
of your homeland—
winter-plaid material
seeping from the darkness,
remembering your frozen
touch when you passed it
along to me.

when i left you,
i had to eat rosary beads
to keep you hidden beneath
the gauze of my flesh; to
suffocate unanswered visions
through muzzled body bags.

we were sacrificial,
standing only inches tall
as we took golf clubs to our
hearts with inches from
our lives. sunset dripping
over the blood we wasted
fucking our way into anarchy.

we were exploitations of
each other. secrets burned
24

from search; love poems
ripped from our veins and
left barren in the snow.

but you are not new to
this. there are other
martyrs from your past
that remember you fondly.
they have been naked for
so long, clinging to your name,
framing memories of you with
bones of their ribcages, but you
have moved on to your next victim.

we are not the end of a movie

when my plane took off into the air,
there was no camera behind me,
no fade to black, no credits rolling
up to tell us the parts we played
in each other lives. we were

only left with the drifting delirium
you had lured me into, creating
apocryphal manuscripts out of
broken typewriter keys; typesetting
emergencies, like the night you
huddled against me. remember?
how your body quaked from the
cold as we watched ghosts dance
around our window from you humming
melancholic love songs, whispering
dreams between the notes.

the next morning we had our
coffee in silence, shadows
intertwining as we shook off
the break of character we exposed
each other to. lost in the sacrifice
we could not make, but we were
ready to return to anarchy the same night.

we were like children, lost in the
idea of attachments to each other,
afraid of how easy we would break.
our fragile arms held each others
names when we were together, letters
twisting between our fingers as we
moved further into the snow. the cold
warming us back from our addictions.

ashamed as i am, it took years for
me to realize that we are not the
end of a movie, so i took my typewriter
out into lawn and set it on fire, frustrated
with knowing it could only type your name---
each letter engraved on slivers of paper.

this poem is an apology letter to the both of us,
for how far i allowed us to go; for forgetting
that some parts of ourselves need to
remain buried. and though i have
forgotten how you look, my skin
still trembles when i remember your taste.

Sleepless

Some nights remain sleepless, so I watched you as
anotherworld drifted your subconscious away from
me. There was grace in your breathing as your
chest rose and trembled down. Such is the
passion no one really thinks of.

There's innocence in sleep, at least that is what I see
when watching you lie beside me, eyes
shattering about violently at each still
movement that is made. Some haloes never
invade us as we stream off into the sanctuary
of ourselves. But that's merely my mind
wandering, maybe one day it'll get lost
among the 4AM fog, what sights it should
see.

The darkness won't last long; it's unfortunate really.
How I'd love to drown in the oceans of your
eyes as you sleep just to see where the waters
take me along your dreams. Though wishes
are a false gift of hope; you'll wake up soon
enough when the sun is barely touching your
toes.

You'll awaken and slide off into the next dive—the
spiffy life that took time and caution to build.

A simple infatuation would not be allowed to demolish the years of being a ghost. And that's all it ever was, a simple ghost with a simple life making memories to be forgotten when you arrive at my door. A bit extensive to say the least.

Memories are as interchangeable as dollar bills. There's not a soul who can live without them; their presence keeps the disorder about while we string along shot of happiness we want to keep. Such a feeling is a Benjamin in the wallet, hard to get but you never want to let it go once you have it.

This is my silence; the faithful understanding of a differing belief. How terribly tragic the circumstances are, but what is one to say to the determined?

I can hear the birds fluttering about, such dreadful creatures this early. The alarm clock will sound in hour or so, right on the hour as per usual. You never would stray off the schedule. It's simply not you. One does get tired of the usual; of the schedule.

You told me you turned wishes into bombs and I've
        been waiting to feel earth erupt with the coins
        I tossed into your wells.

I don't hand out the past for a cup of cheap coffee.
        There are pieces of 25cent newspaper filled
        with manifestos of our history beneath my
        ribcage. Some things are impossible to release
        into the caverns holding archives I never look
        at.

There's no life in between plans, and there's a future
        out there I've yet to see; yet to experience. It
        was never my intention to get caught up in the
        structure of life. I only follow cracks on
        asphalt, thumbing through each moment as it
        comes by.

When you find yourself, look for me. I'll be
        somewhere on a depraved highway.

Maybe then we can make the moon burn.

Waiting

he stares at the stars, his prayer wafting through
them.

waiting for something to hear it.

striving, meditating,

patience minimal

for we are unable to understand ourselves.

Patience never had to know God

to keep the bruises from

hurting.

Farewell

izzy had to bury his dog this morning;
forced to watch his friend drip every
last breath onto the cold concrete,
wrapping him in old sewn up blankets
that barely kept winter at the door.

fingers drizzling beads of sweat,
writing together like prayer beads,
chanting internally, *i love you*, as if
the inevitable could be put off for one
more day. but izzy does not know how to
love, would be better off learning to
hug the ocean of people that slowly
bled him to remain still, only apologizing
for not being able to give his friend comfort,
body quivering at the dying animal.

flames pale beneath his skin as
they silently say their peace in
hopes to meet in another life.

December 24th, 2007

The rain was thick outside,
like the droplets were never
there and a single stream of
water never ceased. It was a
dull roar which lingered
amongst the smell of weak coffee—
the kind of air overdrawn with
pie and cigarettes, and the
only noise was of the clatter
of people, plates and forks.

I was walking out to my car,
street lamps busted, and I was in
the last spot available. I could
hear it around me, beneath this
avalanche of water, silence. They
say silence is deafening, but
it's really only a quaking murmur
waiting around. And in this
circling concerto of earth he stopped
me, gun drawn to my head, the
cold barrel imprinting itself. He
didn't have to say a letter, you
could see it in him. A wallet,
some cash, anything to make this
deal worth it. He had an addiction

to feed and it was scratching at the
the caverns of this throat, to scream
to his one god, "save me from…" But
he never knew that he needed saving. He
showed fragile pebble teeth, the only
thing you could see on him in this mess. Not
a bad guy at heart, his hands trembled like
an earthquake, and it wasn't from the
cold air whipping the nakedness of his face.

The rain was still an overburden,
gun was still shivering underneath,
and his hands have torn acres of land,
by the simple shakes and twitches. He
never said a word, only stared at me
with a look of "It's just how things
go, man. No hard feelings." Between
the both of us, he carried the greater
amount of terror in his body. And
though I was afraid, a part of me
wondered, if I were to die, would
I have seen God. Every day, people
are cutting Him out to hear his voice
as it grows fuzzier with each minute. Would
I have seen God? Like the world's
heartbeat my hands began to tremble,
the hummingbird in my chest flapped
it's wings so fast I could barely stand on

my feet. I grabbed my wallet, slowly,
and knowingly, gave him my last three
dollars of the year. It was an empty
shell he ran off with. This was the universe

Hunger

i see him digging through the trash as
i fill up my car; rose stems for fingers
digging for the little crumbs we take
for granted. his eyes were filled with a
weariness only the desperate would
understand, the hunger fueling his
frenzied search amidst the cold air.

i've seen him before, every morning
under the freeway, sleeping through I-45
traffic and construction. the workers
ignore him, knowing there is no
other place to welcome him.

this man digs through torn credit card receipts
and spoiled yoohoo cartons, only to find
hunger deep within the bottom of the bag.
body quivering, he turns to wander off.
sleep should come to him soon, but what
comfort is there in slumber when the
frozen air attacks you? i shake the final
droplets of gasoline into the tank and
grab my uneaten lunch. fragile fingers
snatch the meal away. saying nothing,
we depart with minor comforts.

our eyes were bright

his voice grabbed me by my spine,
spun me round so hard, my heart lost
sight of the world, stealing the last
inches of breath carried in my lungs.

I held on tighter than his ghost,
neglected by paper-thin voices
and fevered visions. the sky had
never been so calm before. so it goes.

Meditation

she sounds like a new war, a mantra
trickling
    down
       the minds
            of an
       older
    braver
world
subliminal whispers riding through
the ears of the abyss, of addiction

summer is all love,
relived in its heat.

and so she is a most welcome distraction
making her presence known and shattering
the boundaries we've set in
as if some new carnal idea has forced itself upon us.

we looked back at the radical, the meditation that
made sense to them,
embraced it, and a generation was reborn in it—

such is the nature of the radical love.

Communion

ya'll muthafucka's need jesus like i need
the psalms to fill the holes i created. it
took years for us to realize that our lord
and savior was a centerfold, ripped from
a hustler bible; to believe that the
communion wine tastes sweeter when
there's sin involved.

our prayers are tossed out like the morning
trash because it's the only hope we can
cling too; our salvation for a 15 minute
break in life, the same smoke break that
god dreams of. sometimes you have to
work to be holy; to learn to understand.

so we pole dance in the name of jesus as he
cuts our grass; fiddle with a few rosaries and
allow the path of righteousness to burst
on our faces because we believed that
genuflection kept the darkest bill collectors away.

it was only the temporary manna to
keep us silent, to tow us along a bit
further. wafers fill our hands as we
wait for the landlord to call—his
voice as ominous as the myth.

Wet Dreams

we stood naked under fizzling street lights
asking for blessings on the sins we were prepared
to commit; hands crawling on my heart, the beast
vibrating, ready to erupt underneath cold flesh and
silent fingers. but the mind is simply a martyr to the
senses, praying to the stars while he strangles
wet dreams of sadism into my eyes.

smoke lingers as he takes me to see god,
to learn to forget myself. we all carry the
wisdom inside us, designing our own micro-
catastrophes while etching the solutions somewhere
in our body so we never have to look at it, never
have to realize that most answers lie within us.

he is my seductress, though he has aged; only
temporary cotton balls to fill the empty spots
of my veins on nights i couldn't cope. but these
are not the blissful addictions i have been promised.
they are only a few cheap thrills that lack the
ability to repair me, only there
 until tomorrow when i have to return.

The Edge

we clench fists into dirt,
praying for mother nature
to wash away our sins; to
wipe the tears from our
cheeks after we fall.

our ears have not picked
up on her voice; our souls
have not been soothed
over by the songs of her
winds brushing her children.

she sat in front of me, eyes
doused in the salt of her tears;
she fell in love with jack but
needed more than a bottle to
carry the weight of her heart.

some families are incapable
of being whole; their children
become lost in the abyss, following
the droplets of what's left
but never gather enough
to connect them.

healing is a luxury. we
stretch our presence
across our home; it lays
thin across the floor, pushing
further to the edge.

The Size of a Fuckin' Knuckle

She walked in the office, gold ring on
her finger shining against the sun
from the window, diamond the size of her
fuckin' knuckle, but it never fit who she was.

There were wards between her wrinkles;
withered petals from years of living in
a cocaine addiction, but her degree was
only a few steps away. She has worked
years to achieve this much in life, as she
tells me, words spilling from her tongue.

Her eyes poured so much water that
plants could make a home there; spread
their roots through her veins and count
the days she's got left before her body gives out.

I'm watchin' her mouth move, gettin' faster and faster,
and I know she's about to break down; about
to curse the ages of waitress jobs and shitty
bar tips just to feed her children and a man
that can barely look at anything other than her.
she was crawling her way to the final cliff
before descending into the end of a failed
educational career.

I understand where she's coming from; understand
that there are just some days you got to hold
the last penny in your pocket because you don't

have much else. Short change and cut corners
because there's a bill collector around the corner
waiting for your next paycheck like a fuck-up
boyfriend needing bail money.

More often we make a bad choice that forces
us to grab at the Manna from the sky-desperate
to make it through to the next month. I look at her,
realize that we're both in the same world. We're both
just surviving on what we borrowed, living on
what the bank allows us on an overdraft. Praying,
though we know there's only the representative on the
phone to hear our sins. We're not so different. And I
tell her much like I've been told in the same way,
because I'm not in a position to help, only to inform,
"I'm sorry, but there's nothing else we can do."

Maybe We Were Children

When the leaves stole our
imagination in the Autumn,
and the river turned into
 a street corner full of
cities in its cracks, the
jazzman's solemn trumpet
graces the footsteps of
our past as we swam
into rising waters. Someone
called out for us, we heard
them, but our ears never
picked up on their
voice. Maybe we were
children, sitting in the
cool Autumn river, our
past just floating around
us. But we are ghosts,
and ghosts never carry a past.

Repo

i lit a cigarette as i watched them,
morning stillness disrupted by
the noise of their engines, roaring
to keep the sun barely visible. they
latch onto her, no caress to their
touch, and rip her off the pavement
and onto the warm asphalt, tires
screaming as they stole her.

such a shimmer of carelessness
is hard to watch as i puff the
last little bit of nicotine into
myself, a little courage shooting
through my heart as i greet them.

they let me gather my things. felt-
covered seats brush against me
as i remove myself from her. the
man takes my keys, says have a
good day for the sake of customer
service. politics reaches in every
corner of our universe, and little
politeness is a part of living.

my things and i gather on the side
of the road as we all watch them

drive off, solemnity dissolving.

the sky is aimless tonight

uncle jack nestles
along my tongue,
soothing watered-
down visions of tow
trucks and past-due
cars. i use the notices
as coasters to keep
from wasting paper.

you can tell a repo-
driver anything, but their
souls are fully invested
in their jobs. that's all
you can ask of them.

the sky is aimless tonight.
it's silence soaks up the
shivers of the next morning
as i wriggle out the final
drop of unspoken prayers.

there's strange days ahead.
they'll find me one day, cradled
beneath unfinished bombs
digging into spilled imaginations.
they're only obscured by time because
words age faster than we do.

she'll rise again tomorrow,
the abyss will have never
existed; addiction will have

been burned away. he'll
simply be another momentary
lapse of understanding, the
paradise not yet reached.

born into this

we carry tracking devices in our pockets---
electronic typography drafting gps
coordinates to the next open servers while
we order $6 coffee in a big gulp glass to
keep our hearts racing; our minds alert with paranoia

this is a culture of business, guns
waiting at our waist, hair fingers
ready to pound suspicion with a right
to mass market bullets filled with
so much self-importance that it
trickles down to our children. they
become desensitized through foreign
born social distrust of all things living.

Gutting cartoons from their bellies, we
train them to be mini-adults as they
play U.S. invasion with dollar-tree
assault rifles, shooting pretend bullets
into their terrorist friends at the park.

but we are simply born into this
thing of existence, infinity
bent in half as we send prayers
to desolate angels. future sins
absolved as we speak tongues

at the next tv funeral because
we're cute like that; because we're good people.

Street City Blues

I.

The dreamers have all left. They dove into her abyss
        last night, allowed the morphine to strangle
        wet dreams into their veins. We're all so
        appreciative of strange donations, never
        realizing the danger of the strings that snag
        themselves along for the ride. But that's what
        god intended, to control without using
        control.
We are all children grasping at the manna of our debt,
        wishing that today would regress into old age.
Who marched upon Wall Street wishing to change
        the new low price of the higher ups. Social
        media flattened with angry mobs, filled with
        hopes that have been wasting in the backs of
        our skulls. Posted in case you didn't feel like
        showing up.
America has just enough acid in her breasts, squeeze
        every last drop of liberty over the penniless
        who promote the real rights of the people—
        who try to remove the price tag from our
        bodies.
She must protect the core of American values, Gatsby
        is so far lost now.

II.

The earth is rancid now. We've fallen into the same
        trap again. The trap of fiscal responsibility—
        the trap for money.

We manufacture peace symbols into t-shirts and
super-soakers to protect the privacy of our
property only to watch five year olds shoot up
their friends and siblings because death is an
American right. It's unfortunate the
government is merely open for business, what
money it would take to make it private.

Blood is what makes the grass grow, it's what keeps
the heart of the country beating as it does
today. The massive, veiny beast quaking as its
fed cigarettes and grease while the people
ignore the overtime for videos of twerking
and kittens. It's all too easy to find
distractions.

There was never anything wrong with society; we're
all simply too misinformed to tell our leaders
how to truly run the nation. And that's how
they like it, just keep us all poor and mind-
fucked and life is easy.

Our veins run with mixtures of Vicodin and aspirin
while our televisions hand us the next top
model. The nature of politics is merely an
uncomfortable conversation that's impolite to
bring up anymore. Politically correct is how
the spine is ripped from our voices.

And we're all burning for the answer, we simply
don't know how to ask while the ones who
can present the question are ignored as simple
artists for attention.

Flag burners are attention seekers while the poets are
the real prophets. Praise Hosanna the bullet
has been dodged. The heart attack hasn't
ruptured us yet.

III.

The past is simply a superior time. The past of
   beating slaves and learning to overcome the
   racism that is simply being hidden behind the
   closed conversations at the dinner table.
We had prophets then, prophets who were with us;
   held our hands as we learned from the
   mistakes we'd love to forget. But the absence
   of history leads us into the cycle again. To
   argue that it is not important is to argue for
   ignorance.
Freedom meant something then, the news meant
   something then. Journalism was more than
   160 characters posted every second. In so few
   words, headlines tell stories, but that is who
   we are.
There's a blindfold over our brains, the attention
   spans we carry can only handle seconds of
   information before moving on to the next big
   thing if we can afford it.
But that is merely part of the problem. We're all
   focused on the past, the future will never see
   our faces. It'll only see what's left of us,
   maybe put us out of our own self-destructive
   existence.
We'll have forgotten ourselves by then. We'll be the
   new cult next door laid out as examples of
   what happens to convenience.
We drive the nails through the earth's palms, that is
   the stigmata we carry.

politics is an addiction—the
communion of which all our
dissonance becomes one.

we pump oil in our veins to keep
the blood from ruining the caffeine.
the news says America is a business;
that it's a god-given right to starve
the workin' folk. the wealth needs to grow.

television is the swastika of which
we pray, helping the novacain run
through our streets. making us believe
that the doves in our hearts are broken;
that suffering is the key to knowing god.

silence is the weakness we share
as we slice open our chests and expose
our peace in hopes of change, but
our protests are simply poetry on the
bathroom wall, exiled with a broadcast.

Go Back to Sleep

He reads Facebook in the morning with a cup of hot oil, preparing himself for the day of unrest. Fluorescent lights glare against the scratches on his glasses as the lava trudges along his tongue, three or four fast clicks on the internet. It is these slow moments that allow him to remain in sync with himself before opening the door to his office and allowing the new generation of car loans for education.

Liberty is education. Liberty is the ability to become educated and better yourself as a human being; to make yourself more attractive in the working world. Education is the debt you accrue within four years because you didn't know that you have to pay loans back. Student loans are not free money to pay the rent. Not the government's way of saying "you're broke, let me help you." People everywhere brush off a borrowed amount believing they will pay it later but they never take into account the bitch that life is; the vengeance that drips from her lips as she realizes that you're having too much of a good fuckin' time.

He sees them too often; the students, who go to school, switch degrees because they haven't reached the $57, 000 limits to borrow and go to class professionally. They graduate eventually, either when they feel it's time to move on with their life or when their dear friend Uncle Sam pushes them out the fuckin' door with that pile hanging over them. They walk across the stage, degree in hand and right into the unemployment office because Sallie Mae is whipping their ass for their validated learning experiences.

There's juice in her veins; the bankers force her to drizzle it over the American population to keep them quiet as the kids take the only possible help they can get. Education isn't something given by god, only manufactured by businessmen. Compete. Attract more clientele into your esteemed college for a few dollars from the government; the students will cover it later. Call distant mothers and back-broken fathers into the education field and tell them to treat it like a job, that there's some money in it for them. They plaster advertisements for false federal Pell grants and the American public believes it. And why shouldn't they? The morphine's on them all; they're asleep and the snores are unheard.

The bankers tell him that's okay. Let them sleep and pay a few hundred dollars a month because they're responsible adults. They make the choices.

The freshmen students all wander in. Their innocence moves him, but he stays quiet for he needs to make some cash to pay for the degree sitting on his wall. How much will they owe? More than the affordable care act.

Ghosts

we fold ghosts into coins and
place them in our pockets, knowing
that some memories are too
forgiving to forget. but still we hear
their mantras; the taste of
nickel forced in our throats. they
are the past we are not allowed to
let slip through our fragile hearts.

some angels are desolate yet we send
them our prayers; mail them secrets
of sins try to keep hidden. but they can
only open up so wide before shattering
like glass against the clouds.

fragments stuck to our flesh, we lose
site of ourselves, allowing our hauntings
to break us down, decompose our
thoughts, because we are simply an image.

we are devils with haloes broken from
searching, inner piece not achieved because
we allow ourselves to be plagued by
things we left behind. problems saints
are not able to fix, only the patience
to toss our coins down the wells in
hopes of a better future.

play it as it lays

my world is a bucketful of blindfolds
with strings stretch across the top, pluck
one and listen to the vibrations soothe
over your flesh, caressing the beat of
your heart, the macabre dancing along
our hips, afraid of knowing ourselves.

still i take your hand and let
the sky drip over our awkward
jittering, because i am not scared
of the silent sonata beneath your eyes.

The Gift

i wish i could say time has
slowed down for us, such
illusion is beyond us. the
years have passed between
us, and i have lived through
forceful grasps of monotony
never
leaving
until you slid through. we were
underground love affairs spray
painting poetry onto dingy walls.
a broken manuscript that only
fire could fix, and as i look at
the art we engraved into each other,
i can only think that you were
the gift i had been longing for.

Nameless

we're blind pilots, you and I;
wandering nameless until we
dove into the weathered oceans
of our eyes. i still lay among
piles of insecurities, praying for
life to return to them.

my ears stopped listening
to the stars; i wanted to get
so far lost that i'd hear your
breath again. i was only a box
carrying .25 cent newspaper
kept alive on a shelf beneath
my chest because some parts
of the past are too strong to
leave around on the morning table.

when i saw your shores, i put pebbles
in my pockets, crawled through the
matted sands and allowed the cracks
of my feet to spread roots. when i
met you, i gave you a penny because
i heard that you could turn wishes into
bombs, and i've been waiting for
the loudest bang my earth has ever encountered.

Eden

i fucked your ass last night; fucked
you so hard the moon lost its passion.
i saw the saliva stains on the mattress
as your moans whipped against the
gag. you were kinky like that.

fucking your ass felt like fucking
a garden. i don't know what that
means aside from, "hey, you're
pretty." as creepy as it sounds.

the word pretty is eerie in its
own nature. the stoners and the
perverts use it, at least that's what
god said on our last conversation.
we're an estranged couple, god and i.

he always had a way of imagining the
world, but our words got tangled. he was
tossing bullets and I tossed beer bottles to
get the point across. intoxication is the key
to anyone's soul and god was an alcoholic.

he said all the pretty girls came too late. several
flowers were busted up by the shifty phallus of
the lord. i suppose one does change over
the years, even the rulebook has to have
amendments sometimes. i never dreamed
of them, the orgies in heaven that took place.

when we finished, the moon

changed color to match our exhaustion
from the rapture we shared under it. climax
spent as we descend into the restful
drunken abyss, our own tribute to our own eden.

Let the healing bleed through

we send our prayers in hopes the
monsters will remain in the
shadows; burn our bridges to heaven
when they start to swarm around us.

i sent my prayers with you
that morning you were coming
home; stuffed them all in a
text and let the words ride
electric currents to get to you.

you told me he flashed his penis,
about his hands rubbing along your
thighs as open fields swam by
the windows. persistence in his voice,
he made your bones tremble.

i sat at the other end of the screen,
sending more words through the
stiff keys, fingerprints etching into
the keyboard out of anger.

my fists could shatter mountains,
unscarred knuckles hungered to see
teeth splattered into the wall. instead
they held your hand the car ride home;

allowed for stars to form between our
fingers—constellations we use to
find each other because not all things
are burned away at dawn.

i drew you closer when we got home,
held you as a lover should so i could help
the healing bleed through. it takes time
for moments to become illusions; the same
distance it takes for our fingers to reach
gods lips when we're desperate, but there
is still hope here, and you're worth every
new stitch that lays itself along our path.

foreign as it may be, my fingers know
how to return to you when we're lost.

Absolution

our words were too small
for our hearts. our stories
merged and became
unmarried licenses spray
painted around the bones of
our ring fingers. that
was all we could hope
for. matrimony is only
a god-given right.

i wrote our vows
in fire; wore the ashes
on my forehead to
absolve the sins of my
past life before we engraved
ourselves into each other.

when i proposed to you,
we were criminals tearing
at the nature of society. our
love was not human enough;
we were not human enough.

i never grew into the holiness
i had wanted to become. there
was still a guitar left burning
that i have yet to hear.

I took your hand and etched
these words onto your your
heart because i still sweat

nightmares on the good days,
and you've been the only one
to soothe the grease from my
veins; to keep the dissonance alive.

Waiting for Our Ears to Grow Dreams

it took years of navigating under the
moon to understand that some prayers
can only be answered by looking
inward. that's how the messiah wanted it.

i pulled a feather from my ear,
plucked its spine into a stem
and waited for the petals
to drip onto the floor.

it took miracles for me to stop
listening to the stars; to allow
myself the insecurity of getting
lost in the currents of your pulse.

its beat smoothed over the fractures
of my dreams. i had been wandering
nameless for too long. i forgot that
love was merely a wet dream; that
magic doesn't simply burst into life.

Weasel is a writer and overall degenerate poet. He received his Bachelor of Arts in Literature at the University of Houston-Clear Lake and has been blowing up the poetry scene ever since. This Vagabond poet has had the fortunate opportunity to release a full length poetry collection titled Ashes to Burn through Transcendent Zero Press. He has also self-published a small chapbook titled Y'all Muthafucka's Need Jesus. His third book, Cigarette Burns was released Spring 2015 by Kool Kids Press. Weasel has appeared in an indie documentary titled Something Out of Nothing (S.O.O.N.) directed by Mitchell Dudley. His writing has been accepted in several anthologies, some of which include: Houston's Harbinger Asylum, San Jacinto College's Threshold, Permian Basin Beyond 2014,Hunger For Peace, Everything on Earth is Huge and We're All On It, Ginosko Literary Journal, Kracks, Crazy Concrete, Boundless 2015, Di-Verse-City from the 2012, 2013, 2014 & 2015 Austin International Poetry Festival.

He fell into the publishing world after a couple years of releasing the growing literary anthology Vagabonds: Anthology of the Mad Ones. The anthology is still going and continues to feature several talented writers and artists in the community. Weasel Press grew from the idea that we're all mad artists, and is now home to several wonderful individuals. The press has spawned a few other literary journals and continues to be a thriving force in the world of writers.

Some of Weasel's influences include: Hunter S. Thompson, William S. Burroughs, Arthur C. Clarke, Allen Ginsberg, Jack Kerouac, Clive Barker, Thomas Mann, Virginia Woolf, F. Scott Fitzgerald, Kurt Vonnegut, John Ashbery, Anis Mojgani, Buddy Wakefield, Andrea Gibson, H.P. Lovecraft, James Joyce, Nathanael West, Sylvia Plath, and Hubert Selby Jr.

You can catch Weasel at the Websites listed below:

http://poetweasel.weebly.com
http://systmaticwzl.tumblr.com
http://www.facebook.com/poetweasel
http://www.twitter.com/systmaticweasel
http://www.youtube.com/user/systmaticwzl

More Titles from this Author

Ashes to Burn
Published through Transcendent Zero Press

Cigarette Burns
Published through Kool Kids Press

The Hell Inside Us
Published through Earl of Plaid

Acknowledgements

Adam was published in the March 2015 edition of Crazy Concrete, published through Kool Kids Press

Byzantium was published in the 2014 Winter edition of Harbinger Asylum, released by Transcendent Zero Press.

Communion was published in the 2014 Winter edition of Harbinger Asylum, released by Transcendent Zero Press.

Falling Among Stars was published in the early 2015 edition of Ginosko Literary Journal.

Fedora was published in To Hold A Moment Still, released through Transcendent Zero Press.

Liminality was published in Hunger for Peace.

Repo was published in the March 2015 edition of Crazy Concrete, published through Kool Kids Press.

You was published in the March 2015 edition of Crazy Concrete, published through Kool Kids Press

www.ingramcontent.com/pod-product-compliance
Lightning Source LLC
Chambersburg PA
CBHW030154070426
42447CB00032B/1191